MEMORIES

OF

THREE

WOMEN

Memories of Three Women

Copyright © 2013 Bernard Dennis Boylan

First Edition, February, 2018

MEMORIES

OF

THREE

WOMEN

BERNARD D. BOYLAN

Marion

A novella

Bernard Dennis Boylan 2017

Rotterdam, 1940

MEMORIES OF THREE WOMEN

Preface:

It's hard to believe that a depressed 63 year-old man like Bernie, driven out of business by the state and considered washed-up by many, could possess so much unharnessed, misdirected energy. The stories of "Memories of Three Women" happened in the same year, 2002. Afterward, because of too many long hours of writing, a sleep lag, friction at Pondside, moving, and vicious rumors, no female would accompany him until "Braveheart" in 2008. We've dated ever since.

#1: Marion: This is a true story of an attempt at friendship that eventually succeeded. It was written from 15 year-old memories of the unhappily divorced, disillusioned author, who lacked dating or conversational experience and tried too hard to date this woman. The first draft could have been interpreted as a stark "hatchet job," because it ignored the point of view of this talented now-deceased widow. Female readers wouldn't like her treatment. So a subdued version with a conducive, but true, conclusion is presented. Her first name was switched and the family name isn't provided.

#2: Mustang Sally: A fictional story of beautiful dancers, two of whom Bernie had a crush on, even after his daughters warned him. An injury provided them with an opportunity to discard him. All names were changed - See its preface.

#3: A Contemporary Dido and Aeneas: A True story of an artist and fellow hiker, who shocked Bernie by her blunt rejection of a compliment. They only dated twice more. In 2016, Bernie searched and contacted her, but she was now very sickly. She disappeared and he doesn't know how to obtain photos to document her brilliant portraits. Except for Brackman, surnames are omitted.

Thanks to the wonderful staff of the Groton Public Library for help on all stories. And to the Noank Historical Society for help on Brackman.

And special thanks to P. Engle for perceptive observations.

MEMORIES OF THREE WOMEN

Marion was Bernie's initial friend with the singles. She loved their dine-outs, parties, and went on occasional hikes. Marion was a former customer of his copy shop, who remembered him; and then occupied him by a question that led to a fascinating but completely squandered year of his life.

"Why don't you go to more singles events?"

"I don't know anyone and I find it hard to make conversation."

After each change in later life, such as retirement, bankruptcy or a move to another town, friends were lost, most permanently. Too many calls to his kids would alienate them. No one else called. He lacked the nerve to cold call others to establish new relationships. Who was he going to call, anyway?

He decided that he needed to make friends, to make contact to relieve loneliness. He remembered Marion's question. Perhaps, she could be a friend; He hadn't dated in years and began by asking her to accompany him to ECSO concerts (Eastern Connecticut Symphony Orchestra). For years classical music was his only affordable luxury. They met in the lobby beforehand and departed separately. She seemed happy at first, but began arriving later and later until arriving just minutes before a performance. While waiting, Bernie talked to everyone in the lobby from sellers of citrus from Florida to boat owners to patrons. But when Marion finally arrived, she hardly talked, was emotionless, and wasn't much fun. Her silence certainly didn't warrant the expense of the tickets. Bernie asked her out several times afterward, but she was busy. He met her briefly on a hike.

Once in a while, Bernie called after supper, and if she wasn't in the middle of a calligraphy project for a wedding, they talked about their life histories.

Marion was born during the devastating bombing of Rotterdam in the May, 1940, German invasion of Holland. At 20, she immigrated to New York City, first working as a secretary while earning a degree in Classics from Columbia. Marion may have paid most of her own tuition? She met her husband Tom, who was studying for a degree in science. They married in June, 1970.

She never talked about the decades between marriage and Tom's death, except about her two daughters. No one knows why he didn't pursue a career in Science. At some point they moved to Southeastern Connecticut where Tom worked as a yacht painter at Mystic Shipyard.

Tom was born in Philadelphia and was educated in a Friends school. The Quaker emphasis on simple living would have been the reason for his later change of livelihood. A Pan American passenger list on the internet showed that at 18, he flew to England in 1958. Did he tour Europe? Is it possible that he met Marion? She immigrated shortly afterward. His sudden death by stroke at 53 in September, 1993, wasn't anticipated and changed the family history. His previous medical reports on blood pressure and cholesterol were excellent; he was thin, younger, and in better shape than Bernie. He was an avid sailor, participated in many regattas, and had just returned from one. No one could explain his death. Of course, Marion was devastated, but resolved to raise her daughters as a single Mom.

Later, Bernie remembered that he, himself, had worked for two months at the same yard, helping two old-timers haul boats out of the water for winter storage in wide painting sheds. In those years, cables, grease, and a winch on an ancient continental truck pulled the yachts into their respective slots. Modern ship lifts are far more efficient. Bernie remembered the large shed that covered the slip where a wealthy family from Fishers Island stored their yacht every winter.

Two fires destroyed the structures of this historic shipyard where the Civil War iron-clad "Galena" was built and where popular Nathan Fish lost everything in a classic management mistake, optimistically taking another chance after so many successful ones. Carol Kimball wrote an excellent piece about his demise. After reading it, Bernie didn't feel so bad about his own decisions and demise.

Marion called to compliment his dancing at a recent club event. So he invited her to the next one and promised to stay with her. She looked beautiful in a flower print dress and star-burst earrings. Bernie had a single dance with a trouble-making "wild geranium," who had the ability to attract men like flies to honey. Throughout the night, Marion smiled, but held him far away on both slow and fast numbers, and left without a hug. Months later, she told him the dance was "adolescent."

He made two visits to Marion's house. Each time they talked on the porch in a terribly cluttered jumble of childhood toys and porch furniture. He was never invited inside and surmised the obvious: it was too cluttered to be shown. The backyard was an uncut, brush-ridden tangle of bittersweet. He could see that the effort of being a single Mom and still pursuing artistic leanings was almost overwhelming.

After leaving, Bernie remembered classroom stories of

the cleanliness of Dutch women—how the interiors and exteriors of houses were meticulously cleaned. Women even scrubbed and polished their doorsteps. Obviously, Marion was a Dutch aberration: so busy in her job, crafts, calligraphy, and motherhood that she didn't have time or take an interest in cleaning and tidying up. Despite the faults of Bernie's ex, she taught him how to "pick up a house." Why didn't Marion encourage her daughters to help?

After years of contemplation, suggestions from others, gathering a few discarded items, and placing colorful prints on the walls, his apartment developed into the best, most comfortable place he ever lived; it was home. His prints ranged from realist to modern ("Good art is good regardless of the period,") They reflected his latent ambition to be regarded as an author, a wish that proved to be futile in future years; he was destined to be only a storyteller.

Now, for the first time he encountered a woman who raved so much over Jane Austen that many years, she vacationed by flying to a JASNA conference in the U.S. (Jane Austen Society of North America).

Bernie decided to look more closely into this Austen phenomenon to learn more about Marion. On one hand, she flew to conferences, but on the other never spoke about education for her daughters. Perhaps, they lacked motivation, or wouldn't pay their own way like Mom?

The net has pages of JANA events. Librarians and the BBC insist that the memory of this genius is perpetuated throughout the English-speaking world and other parts of the globe. The opinion of one librarian is worth considering: the basis for Austen's popularity is the classic Cinderella story of a poor girl meeting "Prince Charming."

The BBC has an article, "Why is Jane Austen trending 20 years after her death?" with quotes:

"a lasting influence on British literature and culture... She's writing about people and their problems, dysfunctional families, why, and even if, women should marry... issues relevant then and... relevant now... She created these characters so brilliantly (that other women writers of the time) aren't worth one sentence of Austen... stylistic brilliance... she's only interested in the psychology, not the image... But in her lifetime she was a completely obscure figure. "

Jane's 41 years (1775-1817) produced four novels: *Sense and Sensibility* (1811); *Pride and Prejudice* (1813); *Mansfield Park* (1814); and *Emma* (1815); and two published posthumously: *Northanger Abbey*; and *Persuasion* (1817).

As a schoolboy, Bernie was aware of these classics but consigned them to girls and failed to have any interest until retirement when he dated Marion. No one else had possessed so much passion about a writer to fly to distant conferences. One of Bernie's daughters said Jane was too convoluted. The other thought Jane was too dry, and took too long to get to the point.

Bernie, himself, thought that Austen portrayed orderly civilized life among the landed gentry of 18th century England, not the brutal long hours and child labor of the working class during the Industrial Revolution. So her portrayals, though popular, are distinctly distorted pictures of conversation and psychological feelings, with little discussion of landscape, or images, or the repercussions of Adam Smith's laissez-faire on England.

Bernie never studied the history of feminism, but realized that Jane strongly promoted change; change that 200 years later would culminate in the feminine revolution in the U.S. Certainly, this attracted readers.

The sample he selected was an overview of *Emma*, Jane's fourth text. To an outsider like Bernie, the novel contained so many characters and voluminous plot twists that it resembled an 18th century English soap opera or a long-winded fairy tale such as *The Once and Future King* by T.H. White.

One commentator wrote that "morality-characterized by manners, duty to society, and religious seriousness-is a central theme of her works." Many readers harbored a nostalgic wish to return to these values.

Stephen Dobyns, a respected author, interjected his feelings about Austen in With Franz and Jane, a short story in his collection called, *Eating Naked*:

"Janet stopped reading Jane Austen—the subject of her Ph.D. dissertation-and began reading Kafka. The fact that Gregor Samsa awoke to find himself transformed into a gigantic insect was almost reassuring. Hey, he was lucky. It could have been worse."

"Kafka is telling us not to make plans ...He's telling us that beyond our world of illusion is a world of hard truths, ...free will is a phantasm ...Anything can happen at any moment. Never sit with your back to the door."

Most male seniors in Bernie's plat make few plans. They, like him, live day to day. It's so wonderful to be free, not captive to a woman's whims, or subject to leaf -raking, cutting grass, snow shoveling, or "Driving Miss Daisy" and able to formulate a fresh routine for each day.

Years later, he wondered if his lack of physical or financial attributes as compared to the "Prince Charmings" in Austen's books had caused Marion's disinterest. Or did she consider him an emotional lightweight, who lacked intelligence? At this point, he didn't care; he was tired of poor treatment!

A report about Marion said she got excited over local cultural events; however, this never happened when he took her out. On the contrary, she remained extremely cool, way too cool for Bernie so he omitted plans for future events and didn't buy any more symphony tickets.

Their next to last meeting forecasted the end of the dates. On two consecutive nights, he took her to the ECSO and a festival at the Nature Center. At the Center, they talked with another couple, she had seconds on everything, and seemed to enjoy herself until Bernie repeated two stories from the previous night. She re-fused a lunch invitation and left without a kiss, hug, or handshake.

Bernie thought, "Why am I torturing myself with this woman? There must be others with warmth." He need-ed more life in his life and didn't ask about her feelings or health. But looking back, she was overtired, came from a reserved background, didn't want to hurt his feelings so soon after rejoining society, and perhaps, simply wanted a respite from her labors at home.

When he said goodbye at the next concert, he repeat-ed a speech going through his mind. "You're the only woman that would go out with me. The rest treated me like a cripple. Thanks. I'm going to give you a big hug." That was that.

Over the next three years, Bernie dropped out of the singles, finished many books, and moved. More often now, he and Marion called one another. Their conversations got longer and longer. They finally appreciated each other's artistic work. She was a friend. And isn't that what Bernie originally sought?

She complimented him on their last conversation, "You're able to have fun doing simple things and don't need expensive gadgets," He wasn't simple by any standard, but except for his divorce, lived daily life as it presented itself. Though it wasn't his religion, he liked the simple living of the Quakers and Thoreau.

When Bernie's mother died in 2008, all of his teenage goals and duties were accomplished and the remaining years were set aside for fun.

After Tom's death, Marion had raised her daughters by being a substitute teacher in an elementary school and sporadic calligraphy. She often complained of the tediousness of long society calligraphy jobs, the concentration involved, and the pressure of deadlines. Others shudder at the mindless repetition. The work wore her down; she was tired.

But she had the Dutch artistic eye for creating colorful patterns around catchy quotations and won prizes in local shows. Bernie could vouch for her mental keenness and ability to get things done. Because of that ability, she remained the leader of local calligraphers for years.

When Bernie complained about his obstreperous Mom, she countered with stories of her own family in Europe. Her brother had dropped out of the rat race and settled on a small farm in central France. He made visits to their mother and reported on her near-fatal heart condition that persisted even after a pacemaker was installed. Marion flew to Holland and France more frequently.

Although Bernie's memory may be faulty, her last flight to Holland may have been necessary to participate in a Dutch euthanasia procedure requested by her Mom. This action happens far less frequently than publicized; and only when bureaucratic, religious, and family obligations/ agreements are met. Marion said it only happened twelve times the previous year in a current population of 17 million.

Marion died suddenly in 2015, only weeks after a diagnosis of sarcoma. Since Bernie no longer belonged to the singles, his friends were different and he never heard her name mentioned again. It's up to the daughters and granddaughter to carry on the beautiful art tradition of Dutch painters, like Rembrandt, Vermeer, Brueghel, Bosch, and later, Van Gogh. One would hope that besides reading Jane Austen's works, they have also adopted the cleanliness tradition of their forbears.

Bernie salutes Marion's stubborn resolution. After Tom's death, she held her course and did the best she could with what she had.

Mustang Sally

the Dancing, Dating Sessions of Seniors

A Novella

Fiction

Bernard Dennis Boylan 2011; 2017

Preface:

In *Mustang Sally*, Bernie writes about seniors he encountered during a troubled year of dancing; and the
idiosyncrasies of participants, which undoubtedly persisted for the rest of their lives. All names are changed.
The story is fictitiously based on incidents that happened a decade ago. Since then, he's lost track of
everyone.

His short dancing tour was ruined by a rotator cuff injury and vicious rumors of mental illness. Writing this novella is a lot less bruising than the actual experience.
Years later, Bernie changed his sleeping patterns to earlier bedtimes, rather than post-midnight, stopped
searching for pretty women, and happier times re-
sumed.

The protagonists:

Sally: A feisty petite brunette dancer on a quest to find security in a rich husband.

Mary: The tall blonde manager, who lured Bernie into dancing and broke his heart that summer.

Ron: The fireplug whose critical outbursts were hilarious.

Tami: The determined rich woman, who repeatedly drove long distances to find love, but failed.

Don: The butt of jokes, who ignored criticism, vigorously exercised, and finally found fulfillment.

Gray: Sally's sister who needed advice from her older sibling about everything.

Carmen: A digger of financial info that bordered on callousness. She never found a boyfriend.

Raymond: A late arrival who correctly chose to retain his bachelor lifestyle.

Anne: A veteran of three divorces.

Bernie: A recent retiree in a social gospel phase of life, who lacked necessary dating skills.

Ted, a former neighbor who didn't dance, knew Bernie was lonely; and invited him to join a weekly singles club function: a cocktail hour followed by an evening of dancing. Although Ted left after several drinks, Bernie stayed to observe the goings-on. The dancing didn't start until hours later and disappointed, he prepared to leave. But pretty Mary asked him to return. Dancing with this tall goddess would be fun. Next week, Bernie only danced the slow numbers, and Mary grabbed him for every waltz. She was a widow, a manager, and a mentor, "We'll teach you to swing dance." Bernie lost his heart; but was he just a dance partner?

After a hike at Rocky Neck State Park, many of us celebrated Cinco de Mayo at a local sports bar that offered a Mexican buffet and cheap margaritas. We had a great time talking: Don was his usual foolish self, which provoked outspoken Ron, a retiree with an extremely short fuse. He lost patience after three margaritas. Doctors had warned him and others to avoid alcohol.

Well-off Tami, who always turned compulsively talkative after alcohol, told Bernie multiple times, "I have to go slow in my romance with Ron." Many recent tragedies have happened in her family. But she was used to getting what she wanted and head over heels in love with Ron, traveling long distances three times a week to be with him. Bernie wondered, "I hope she won't be hurt again—but if she gave up those damned cocktails, she'd have a better shot at Ron's heart."

We teased cute petite Sally about the terrific dancer she was inseparable from at Cobblestones, a shoreline restaurant. She replied, "It isn't serious; I'm just having fun." Sally's deceased husband was a famous marathoner from Providence College. Before dying, he surprised her with a '66, 4-seat, Mustang convertible.

She kept the car locked up and took meticulous care of it, treating it like a family heirloom. It was old enough to be a classic. She once bragged that it was appraised for more than $30,000. Her nickname was "Mustang Sally," because of the car and the song from the '60s that inspired its purchase.

The singles were a lonely hearts club that socialized so our losses wouldn't feel so bad. The club got us through the aches of empty hours; the good memories of get-togethers helped us cope until the next event.

In early May, Ron led a singles hike around a pond at the end of a long dusty road. Only ten members showed up. White violets bloomed atop the earthen dam. At the end of the hike, the seniors got winded on small hills and wooded ravines. Last Fall Ron had stents placed in his arteries, but was overweight and breathing hard. As we crossed a wet area dotted with boulders, Bernie effortlessly hopped from rock to rock. Someone said, "Look at Bernie-he's like a mountain goat." Within a month, however, his balance disappeared and never returned. The cookout under the trees, afterward, was full of laughter and conversation. The two-hour inter-play between outspoken Ron and silly Don made the event entertaining.

In May the monthly club dance was held. Mary couldn't go but a large number of women were present, far more than men. It's surprising how many widows were so desperate for a man that they recited their personal stories without being asked. One woman's feet were like lead-Bernie couldn't even push her around. Though he danced with other women to mostly slow songs, he missed the closeness of Mary. Bernie left early. His shunning of pleasant, hard-working, loyal, but plain women was one of his worst mistakes in retirement.

Sunday was drizzly. Don and Bernie were the only ones to show up and hiked, anyway. Bernie got to know him better. He was tall, wiry, white haired, and garrulous. He gave hilarious wedding proposals to most of the women in the club; "Oh beautiful Sophie, will you accept my proposal? I'll give you roses every day" They laughed and told him to get serious. After a quadruple bypass, he exercised as much as possible. Don attended almost all of the club events, knew most of the members, and was a walking, talking history of the Singles. Bernie wondered if he accomplished anything substantial in life, or was simply a will-of-the-wisp, floating through the years like so many others?

During the next two Friday nights, Bernie enjoyed the

company and warm closeness of women as we danced at Cobblestones. Sally and Al were inseparable and put on an entertaining show. It was beautiful to watch them dance. Bernie blurted, "You're the two best dancers on the floor!" Sally gratefully acknowledged his compliment. He watched their graceful moves and learned. Al was a retiree with a big pot-belly but was so energetic and coordinated that his skills were admired. While talking during band breaks, Bernie discovered Al was a simple guy. Petite Sally was an excellent partner, and to Bernie's eye, the best female dancer in the club.

When Bernie first arrived at Cobblestones weeks ago, the women gave him quick "on-the-job training." Since then he watched other dancers every week, getting better quickly, but would never approach Al's graceful expertise. Tami and others said, "You're getting to be a good dancer." Compliments were an early boost to his ego, but were eventually detrimental and accompanied by fatigue, led to personal problems.

At 11 pm, Al requested, "Could you play 'Mustang Sally?" His partner loved that song and 'Oh when the Saints.' Petite Sally's feistiness, hard work, and smooth dancing was reminiscent of Bernie's Mom. Going home, he hummed the lyrics so often that he couldn't get to sleep; the emphatic "Ride-Sally-Ride" repeated over and over in his mind. He got up, drank a beer, and finally went to sleep at 2 am. Another late night, one of too many.

On May 31st, Tami arranged a double birthday party for Ron and Mary. The women danced wildly, wiggling their hips, waving their arms, shouting the lyrics, and flaunting themselves on prospective partners like the showy wild geraniums on the wooded trails. Tall energetic Anne was with quiet Dick; blonde Mary with

Bernie; petite Sally with pot-bellied Al; talkative Tami

with Ron; and pert Lou—Lou with steady Joe. The place

was even hotter than the last time. Everyone was

drenched in sweat.

On Sunday a small group gathered at the Mystic rail-

road station for a three-mile hike. After crossing the

bridge, we walked through the historic district, follow-

ing the river until reaching the underpass. Another wild

rose was blooming all along the shores. We drove to a

restaurant for food, drinks, and fun. Anne drank a non-

alcoholic beer after a bleary night at Cobblestones. Ron

bickered with Tami and she gave it back. The happiness

from last night's party didn't last 24 hours!

Don led a hike at Rocky Neck. Afterward, as we ate and

drank at a sports bar, chubby always bubbly Sandi got

hugs and kisses from Don as his new "fiancée." She rel-

ished the foolish attention. Thin Ingrid, a heavy smoker

but good dancer, told us about one reincarnation after another.

The next week the men drank downtown, sharing stories of the women we danced with. Ron told us again, "Tami talks way too much; She's a' chasing me and I'm a' running." Don reached a different conclusion, "Most of the women are independent and just want a few laughs, a good time, and a partner to dance with. They don't want relationships." Who was correct?

In mid-June, Tami, Ron, and Don joined Bernie for another walk along the river. It was too hot and humid to walk but we foolishly tried. The sweat poured off us. We took a break under trees and decided to return to town. At a restaurant on the river, Tami splashed water from a basin all over her hair and face to cool off. She was a rare woman who didn't get upset when her hairdo was mussed up. She still looked pretty. For a retired woman her skin was smooth without wrinkles. Was it due to Botox and a facelift?

On the following weekend, it was obvious that Bernie missed a signal. His friend Mary was lovey-dovey with a new boyfriend. Bernie had a terrible time; there's nothing worse than watching a new boyfriend kiss your old girl! While at the dance, Joe looked lonely because sexy Lou-Lou also had a new boyfriend; Ron and Tami sat separately after arguing. Bernie left early and walked past drunk, crying Tami , "I've had a bad night," she said. "So have I." He couldn't stop his emotions--he was rejected. Why did he trust women?

Six of us hiked in late June. Ron, Don, Carmen, Gray, me, and Raymond, a newcomer. While walking, short friendly Raymond told me about his diet, grandchildren, and home renovations. The river was busy with lots of boat traffic. Blonde Gray, Sally's sister, walked beside me for a mile. "My husband took good care of me until he suddenly died in his sleep and left me with a too-small pension. I can't afford to retire-I'll have to continue working." Gray was lonely, very friendly, had a good shape, but was a heavy smoker. Although Bernie danced with her, he always discouraged Gray because of that habit and an obvious personality mismatch.

In mid-July the gang hiked. Bernie's friends told him the news: when Al wanted to get serious, Sally told him to get lost and he never returned. Mary's love affair had fizzled. Tami got drunk early and spent the rest of the night in the parking lot and bar, trying to sober up. She knew enough to eat and drink coffee to get sober. Most people would be too embarrassed to show up, but she was persistent.

Ron pronounced, "I'm no longer dating or dancing with Tami." Did he want to take Sally out?

When we hiked, the hydrangeas surrounding historic houses were a soft blue. From a chimney, a long-tailed mockingbird repeated songs, a half-dozen times each. Ron and Tami clashed. She bragged about her wealth. Once again, Ron said, "I don't care for her; the chemistry isn't right, and she talks far too much." He was attracted to small Sally and always titillated her with comments about her shape: "Hey, swivel hips!" She loved it and wiggled. Sally wasn't present today, but Bernie warned Ron about her remark at last night's dance: "I'm looking for security in a man." Translation: she wanted a rich husband—Ron didn't qualify.

On random nights, Sally danced with rich prospects but was too obvious to all of them. Her obsession with wealth came from the poor, dysfunctional family in which she was raised. Sally was well provided for by her late husband and was comfortable. However, she loved Ron's teasing and returned for more. Bernie wondered. "Would she be happy with him?"

Unknown to anyone, Tami and Ron met every Wednesday at a local waterfront restaurant. Once, Bernie ran into them at the bar. An intelligent 30-year old blonde sat next to us, drinking pinot grigio while reading the financial pages. Tami couldn't resist bragging, "I just bought blue chips for my portfolio."

Feeling way too smart and smug while walking back to our cars, Bernie brought up something that was none of his business. "Why don't you reconsider Tami: she's pretty, madly in love, and very rich. You're never going to find a perfect woman. If you can withstand Tami's talking, 'your ship has come in!' Tami will take care of you for the rest of your life." Bernie's advice was unso-licited-Ron never forgave him and was no longer a friend.

Mary reconciled with Bernie. In mid-August the gang sat on her deck, laughing at one another. Carmen mentioned a $2000 operation on her dog to remove a sock. We knew she didn't like to spend money. Carmen told us about other expenses, like fencing and a rug, that the dog ruined. Someone mentioned, "Euthanasia." Gray, who was always good for a laugh, guessed, "I don't know about Euthanasia; you should kill the dog!" Everyone roared. Mary, who had a tough week, was reenergized by the laughter and did a little war dance. Bernie talked with her and another about traveling to Europe. She hugged and invited him to hear Irish Music the next day with Sally and Gray. On that sizzling Sunday, his car air conditioning failed. Without it, Bernie drove on I-95 to visit his Mom in Cranston, RI, and then at 6pm, in the opposite direction to Old Lyme, CT. The traffic was so bad that the drive to Cobblestones from Mystic took 60 minutes instead of 35. We sat near the accordionist, who played our requests, concluding with *Oh when the Saints*.

During a club dance, Sally danced with a chunky be-spectacled man, Sally attempted to learn the cha-cha but her partner was dissatisfied. In the middle of the song, he said "Thanks" and walked off. Sally was flab-bergasted, momentarily, but chased after him, yelling "Who do you think you are, Gene Kelly?" We roared.

Bernie started slowly but danced every number with a different woman until midnight. Sandi, one of Mary's friends, complemented him, "You're really coming out of your shell." He drank two beers, ignoring doctor's advice. He bought three rounds for his widowed friends. "Why," they asked? "The other guys are so tight."

Well prepared, he replied, "Old men always treat the beautiful women in their lives." They laughed. After two beers, one woman confirmed, "Mary is seeing another guy. I don't want to see you hurt. You should continue dancing until you find a nice woman."

Bernie's reply was way too simple, "Nothing Mary does will surprise me. I won't be hurt at all." Of course, it didn't work out that way.

Many women asked him to dance, several times with four widows at once. In unison we sang the theme to Mustang Sally, our unofficial club theme song. Many women in the club had let themselves go: matronly with mousy dispositions, could talk only about Florida condos or favorite TV shows, and weren't fun to be with. They looked and acted like grandmothers. Others were pretty, thought young, enjoyed having fun, and got most of the dances.

Bernie told Raymond, "I don't know what Mary sees in me, but I'll take her as long as it lasts. She isn't taking advantage; I'm dancing with a beautiful woman who makes me happier than I've been in a long time. I can take the inevitable rejection, when it comes." In reality, he was as emotionally vulnerable as if a storm approached.

In August a crucial event happened that Bernie didn't realize until later. He went dancing at a tavern with four widows until closing. One guy told him, "You've got your hands full with these women." Too full! Sally and Gray lined up three big glasses of Sam Adams in front of him. He danced every number with a different widow. The only rest was for band breaks. Earlier that evening, he watched a young woman dance with moves that were wild, animated, varied, and provocative. Was she on speed? Or just wild? She whirled her lengthy black hair in a circle or jerked it back to front. The way she pranced around the floor made all the men watch her.

Sally and Bernie got up to dance with her. When he asked for her name, she jerked her head away and pranced to the other side. Bernie had never seen anything like it. Women like her have caused wars. Bernie explained the "Dance of the Seven Veils" to his partners: after Salome danced, Herod said he would grant whatever she wished. She wanted the head of John the Baptist on a platter. So Herod granted her wish. The women each hugged Bernie before leaving.

With the beers Bernie felt no pain and little fatigue; however, the violent arm swings of the twist were repeated too many times. Next morning, he belatedly realized that he wasn't an iron man. When he woke at 9 am, he was lying on the covers in his clothes, the lights were still on, and his left shoulder was killing him. It took forever to put on a tee shirt. Driving was done one-handed. On Monday, he called the local VA. They told Bernie to visit VA—West Haven on Tuesday where a tom rotator cuff was confirmed, but wouldn't give him therapy for weeks! Of course, Bernie recovered after the therapy, but in the meantime, every turn in his sleep woke him up. Between dancing, hiking, writing, and this injury, once again he built up a huge sleep-lag. None of the singles ever called. Sally never understood that dancing caused his injury.

Despite a harsh childhood, Sally had grown up to be normally level-headed 65-year-old widow who cleaned houses for spending money, had a good pension and health benefits from her late husband, lived in Waterford, spent time with grandkids, and volunteered at the library. She loved beer, was the best dancer, was petite, and loved to run fingers through her brown hair. Bernie loved that habit. But she announced that she was looking for a rich husband and Bernie didn't fill the bill. Her obsession with wealth came from childhood and she was the only one that could change. Her snazzy personality was really appealing. Bernie had a crush on her, too.

By October, things had changed. Right away Bernie's doctor knew he was drinking and chewed him out. Because he split with Mary, the clique gave him the cold shoulder. Three times, a pleasant widow, Lily, asked Bernie to dance because he looked lonely, standing in back. Behind him was the club president, deciding whether Bernie was dangerous or not. Sally and Ron had turned on him. Bernie came home before midnight with his head high, his resolve strong, and sober.

Bernie intended to go with the gang on events for exercise, expecting that the fun would resume. It didn't. It
was hard to believe that he had wasted so much time
and effort on shallow, self-interested people. He could-
n't believe that he hadn't made any friends. None of
these women ever called; they were just "party ani-
mals." Even Ron turned on him last night. Twice, he
talked with Raymond. But the clique didn't want Bernie
any longer.

While eating in a restaurant, Bernie loudly chastised
Carmen for not cancelling an invitation. On the way out,
Sally was brusque, "He's a bomb waiting to go off." It
was a cruel remark because he had been a gentle per-
son all his life. Three times this week, she referred to
"your condition," Bernie's mental problem. He should
have asked about "her condition," the foolish pursuit of

wealth. Happy-go-lucky Don solved the puzzle.

(See the aftermath on the next page.)

Aftermath

Americans are not knowledgeable about mental health. One size doesn't fit all. Bernie was treated as a cripple, a troublemaker—everything he did was blamed on this disability. He couldn't have a personality. Others like Sally shot their mouths off every day. Along with a huge sleep lag, hazing caused him to drop his membership in the singles. He was way too open with them and would never recover his reputation.

Raymond called to ask if Bernie was hiking? He enjoyed hearing about dancing and the futile attempts to find a girlfriend. He was smart enough to just talk with women. He enjoyed his grandkids, freedom, and home.

Bernie should have followed Raymond's example, acted his age, smiled at the dating scene, and enjoyed his grandkids.

That winter was the last time Bernie met members. At a restaurant, apologies were forthcoming, but times had changed. Anne married for the fourth time. Tami found a wonderful boyfriend who escorted her everywhere. A harem of women followed Ron's caravan. The last time Bernie saw him, he was churning gravel in a lot in Sally's Mustang with the top down. He died in 2009 after his heart slowly gave out.

People barely noticed, but Don began dancing with the "forsaken" women at club dances. They weren't finicky and had more to offer. When Lily asked Don to visit her condo in Florida, he told his tenants to fend for themselves. For someone regarded as foolish, he was the smartest one of all. Yet he died a few years later. Mary remarried and renovated two houses. Eight years after we met she traveled to Europe. To blunt criticism from his kids, Bernie introduced her. They understood the attraction, but to this day, still think Dad was foolish.

Like most of the women in our clique, Sally searched for a rich husband. If one appeared, the "Women's Financial Network" quickly found a friend of a friend to confirm his status: Divorced? Retired? Home owner? Wealthy? She met a number of candidates but each time, changed her personality and became too serious and mousy; she didn't connect. The men were looking for frisky women. Ha! And Bernie? Why he was just a disposable dance partner!

In 2 Corinthians 12, the apostle Paul complained three times of a thorn in the flesh, but the Lord wouldn't remove it: *"My grace is sufficient for you, for my power is made perfect in weakness. "* One theory is that the thorn alluded to a woman. Bernie persistently struggled to find a pretty woman. With such unreasonable standards and low resources, he searched, fruitlessly. But wasn't he stronger without women? Didn't his writing and intelligence improve; and also his personality? Like Paul, when he was weak, he was strong. Berne's false conceit was disconnected. He accepted his situation and the rest of his life went smoother.

Lyrics to Mustang Sally:

Guess you better slow your Mustang down
Oh Lord what I said now
Mustang Sally now baby
Oh Lord guess you better
Slow your Mustang down hu-oh yeah

You been runnin' all over town now
Oh I guess I have to put your flat feet
On the ground
       Hu! what I said now

Listen!
All you wanna do is ride around Sally
(Ride Sally ride)
All you wanna do is ride around Sally
(Ride Sally ride)
All you wanna do is ride around Sally
(Ride Sally ride) huh
All you wanna do is ride around Sally
Alright (ride Sally ride)
Well listen to this
One of these early morninin's

Hey Wow! gonna be wipin' your weepin' eyes
Huh! what I said now-look-a-here
I bought you a brand new Mustang
A nineteen sixty-five huh!
Now you come around
Signifyin' a woman
That don't wanna let me ride
Mustang Sally now baby oh Lord!
Guess you better slow that Mustang down
Huh! oh Lord! Look here
You been runnin' all over town
Oow!
I got to put your flat feet on the ground
Huh! what I said now hey-a
Let me say it one more time y'all
Now all you wanna do is ride around
Sally (Ride Sally) hu! (ride)
All you wanna do is ride around Sally
FADES...
(Ride Sally ride)
All you wanna

(Lyrics written by Mack Rice, 1965)

MEMORIES OF THREE WOMEN

A Contemporary Dido and Aeneas:

a Novella

Bernard D. Boylan 2017

(Picture in the Louvre
by Pierre-Narcisse Guerin of Aeneas and Dido)

The June 4th five-mile AMC hike at Pine Ledge was shorter than another seven-mile hike offered on Tuesdays. I found my body recovered faster after the short hikes; I only wanted to keep my legs in shape, not run marathons. I got to know the usual hike leader John and Dido, a talented portrait artist, who often teased John to bring along his harmonica to serenade us on the trails. A big deficiency in my education was the arts, so I determined to talk to Dido more often.

Despite only hiking twice at the shore that summer, I got myself up early on September 3rd, ignored threatening rainclouds, and made the forty-minute drive to Colchester to hike with my friends, John and Dido. The hike was a slow easy walk on level trails at a wildlife management area: eight women and five men participated. Sparsely rayed, white, wood asters bloomed low

along the trailsides. We passed yellow fields of different, waist-high species of goldenrod.

The hike was mostly uneventful until we carne around a
sharp corner, went down a slope, and forded a rushing
brook on flat boulders. We came upon the most beautiful display of wildflowers: vivid scarlet cardinal flowers,
bushes of yellow touch-me-nots, and five-foot purple
Joe-Pye weeds. The trail was lined with small wood asters. Sunlight flashed through the branches. It was an
epiphany, a revelation, in the woods. God was broad-
casting that he would take care of me, and a decade later, I'm certain he did. At home I looked up the biblical
parable of the lilies of the field in MT6: 25-34

Do Not Worry

[25]"Therefore I tell you, do not worry about your life, what you will eat or what you will drink," or about your body, what you will wear. Is not life more than food, and the body more than clothing? [26]Lookat the birds of the air; they neither sow nor reap nor gather into barns, and yet your heavenly Father feeds them. Are you not of more value than they? [27]And can any of you by worrying add a single hour to your span of life? [28]And why do you worry about clothing? Consider the lilies of the field, how they grow; they neither toil nor spin, [29]yet I tell you, even Solomon In all his glory was not clothed like one of these. [30]But if God so clothes the grass of the field, which is alive today and tomorrow is thrown into

the oven, will he not much more clothe you-you of little faith? [31]Therefore do not worry, saying, 'What will we eat?' or 'What will we drink?' or 'What will we wear?' [32]For it is the Gentiles who strive for all these things; and indeed your heavenly Father knows that you need all these things. [33]But strive first for the kingdom of God' and his' righteousness and all these things will be given to you as well.

Two weeks later, thirty-one members hiked at Gillette Castle Park in East Haddam, a drive of fifty minutes. I gave Dido a copy of my memoir because she never complained about spinal stenosis, and was always pleasant. The views from the hill, one of the seven sisters, were spectacular: the Connecticut River, the opposing hillsides, and far below, a tiny seasonal ferry making its crossing. We hiked around the former estate on trails and on remnants of the trail bed of a miniature railroad.

On October 29th, the country roads were translucent from the leaves of overhanging branches. It was the most colorful autumn in recent memory.

Dido read my memoir and sent a thank you note within four days. She asked me to visit her. I confirmed the date, and complimented her for not complaining about her illness on our hikes; she was an inspiration to the rest.

Hundreds of blackbirds swirled in unison through the skies- a portent of changes in weather and relationships.

We car-pooled to an old resort community and had
lunch at a high grassy cleared hillside overlooking Salmon Cove, Salmon River, Haddam Neck, the Connecticut
River, and patchwork hillsides on the opposing shores.
Largely unknown, it's one of the prettiest spots in Connecticut. I walked with Dido for long periods and
learned that she studied under the late Robert Brackman from Noank and Madison. She was house-sitting
for a year on the shores of the Connecticut River, hoping to regain her inspiration for painting.

I learned about Brackman at the Noank Historical Society. He was a Russian immigrant who became famous
after painting portraits of Charles and Anne Morrow
Lindbergh. He restricted his portraits to three or four. a
year to allow time for other subjects such as still-lifes,

mannequins, and semi-allegorical paintings. He taught around fifty students each summer. As he wandered around the easels giving advice, ashes from an ever-present cigarette dropped onto his shirt, causing the women to yelp. As he aged the clerical burden became too heavy and he closed his school and taught in Madison.

Brackman

On November 1st, I drove to Haddam, a small town on the River, to visit Dido. The directions were exact—I never would have found the house without them. While past their peak, leaves on the hills were still colorful. The large colonial was on the wide bank of the river. Despite my invitation to lunch, she surprised me with tasty soup and sandwiches. We had a great view of the fast-moving river, powerboats, and a floatplane from the Goodspeed Opera House.

I finally had a chance to ask, "You have an unusual name. How was it given?"

"My Mother was always interested in ancient history. Eventually, she became a history professor at Wesleyan University. According to ancient sources, Dido was a beautiful queen who fled with followers from Tyre in Phoenicia and founded Carthage on a site in what is now modem Tunisia. Parts of the account are in Virgil's Aeneid. The boundaries of the settlement were established by staying within the bounds of an oxhide. Dido cut slips narrow enough to encircle a hillside. The city prospered.

"When fleeing Trojans arrived, she fell in love with their leader Aeneas, After they left to found Rome, she was trapped by public pronouncements of patriotism and loyalty. Rather than submit to a local ruler, she committed suicide by sword and immolation.

"It's a story. Carthage was founded about 72 years before Rome so it's unlikely that Dido met Aeneas. Moreover, she's listed on historical records; he's not. Her story was so popular in the post-renaissance period that it inspired thirteen operas, a damning appearance in Dante's Divine Comedy, dramatized by Christopher Marlowe, and publicized by Goethe's abandoned girlfriend."

Dido was of medium height, wiry, had long sturdy legs, and always wore a white ball cap on the trails. She was pretty but no spring chicken. We talked for hours about our travels. Although I had made several week-long trips in the Army, Dido had traveled in Europe for an entire year. She refreshed many memories for me, such as the manned crossing gates for railroads in rural Germany. We talked about Rodin, about the reclusiveness of Cezanne. I told her about my love for Matisse and Mondrian.

"Wow, that's a switch. Most Americans don't get past Picasso!"

She knew her stuff. Spanish art, especially early Miro, was her favorite. (Next pages.)

Miro: Portrait of a Little Girl

Miro: Self Portrait

Miro: Portrait of Spanish Dancer

Brackman: Jennie

Brackman, the portrait painter, was a big influence on her, even advising her for financial reasons not to get married. She did, anyway, had two children, and something happened? The divorce was so bitter that only now had she reconciled with her children.

She was friendly with two hikers. I laughed over a stunt they pulled during a lunch break: they set up an old-fashioned picnic complete with blanket, wine, sandwiches wrapped with wax-paper, and cheese. The others gasped at their spread.

She said exercise and hiking loosened her spine. We talked for hours until the sun started setting. At last, I had found the companion for whom I was searching.

Dido had a big smile like her namesake and was very intelligent, but it proved to be deceptive. When I tried to compliment her by saying "You're a very interesting woman," she demanded to know why I didn't call her "Beautiful!" I was dumbstruck that a middle-aged woman could be so hung up on the concept of beauty. I didn't want to insult her; I didn't want to lie either. I didn't know what to say. My silence was so painful. The potential romance was damaged by my clumsy compliment. Don't ever call a woman "interesting!"

Soon, I invited myself to Dido's: she was painting the river and hillside with a big straw hat on the lawn under a massive Ash tree. It was so "plein air," so impressionistic. Several times, we met for lunch in East Lyme. She found renewed inspiration for portraits. Her new work was stunning. We inspired each other, but she was already an artist; I was just a wannabe. Dido was a friend who had had many hard knocks in life. Although I tried several times, I couldn't get Dido to drive past Niantic. I never knew why.

Why didn't we pair up? For me, it was a period of tre-
mendous physical and mental exhaustion. I pushed too
hard at too many activities. It took me years to learn to
sleep earlier and reclaim my personality. Dido was so
pissed at my latest book that she warned me not to
contact her, anymore. I didn't call her for twelve years,

Some Aeneas, huh? But looking back, God took care of
me, just as he promised.

A decade passed. Dido moved; Bernie moved, also. In
forthcoming years, both had had problems: She with
her lungs; he with endurance and Pondside residents.

In 2016, while having tea, a cleaning lady made suggestions to Bernie—A picture was needed on a blank wall,
and a scatter rug next to the bed. Finding the rug was
easy. But the picture was a problem. He called two

different friends to trade an early unwanted canvas for two original books of their choice. Neither responded and he presumed no!

Bernie remembered Dido and found her number. After a few questions she remembered him, agreed to supply a canvas, but couldn't drive to meet him halfway. He found out why. After lunch, he found himself in the clustered village of Chester, CT, climbed to the loft, and found her connected to oxygen by tubing extended along the floor. Dido was a life-long smoker. She was shorter, too skinny, had an ominous pallor, with straight gray hair. She knew the danger of smoking, but loved it too much. Dido was ten years older than Bernie.

He remembered her as an agile hiker with a black pony-tail, a white hat, her good friend John and their gag of an old-fashioned picnic in the woods, complete with cheese and wine. She hugged Bernie: for old time's sake and generously gave him his choice of a painting. He had only brought three books and felt like a tightwad. Because he had wanted something simple, he decided to take a smaller painting instead of a large nude.

At home, he mailed four more books of her choice and enquired about the real price of the nude, hoping to offer cash along with books-he didn't want to take advantage of her. But she had terrible difficulty talking on the phone. So he had waited for a letter.

The letter was never received-Bernie called, but doesn't know what happened to Dido; or if she's still alive?

He doesn't know how photos of her brilliant portraits can be obtained. He wanted to document some of them in this story.

Sources:

The Aeneid, by Virgil; translated by Robert Fitzgerald

T.S. Eliot: an Imperfect Life, by L. Gordon

Richard Picemo

Dido

Wikipedia

Seasons of Life, by B.D. Boylan

     (retitled, "God created a Wildflower")

Hard Luck! Soft Landing, by B.D. Boylan

The Groton Public Library

Audubon Field Guide to Wildflowers

The Divine Comedy, a critique by editor Harold Bloom

Noank Historical Society

Appalachian Mountain Club (AMC)

Made in the USA
Middletown, DE
31 December 2020